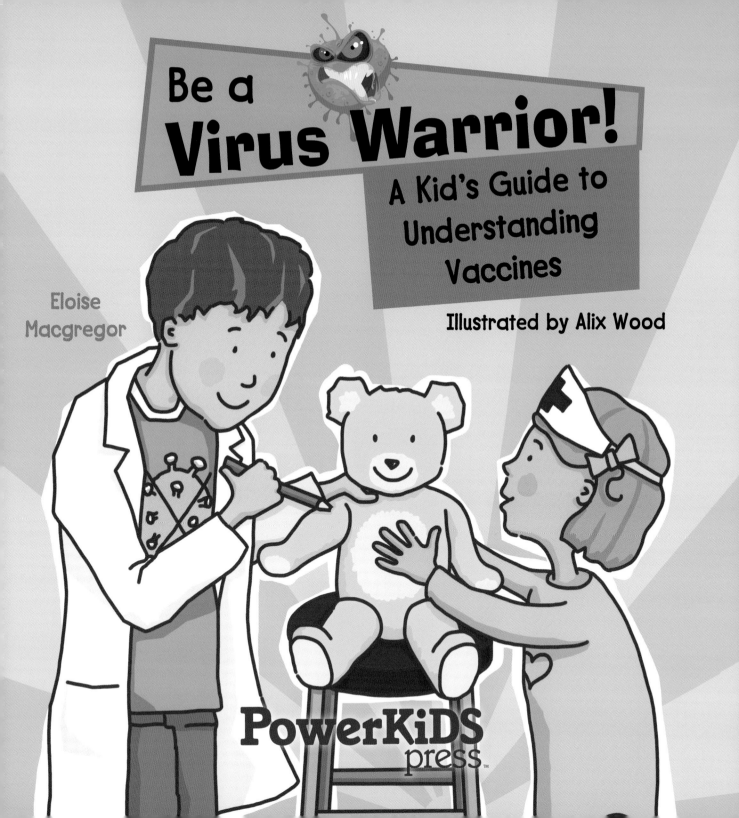

Be a Virus Warrior!

A Kid's Guide to Understanding Vaccines

Eloise Macgregor

Illustrated by Alix Wood

PowerKiDS press

Published in 2022 by The Rosen Publishing Group, Inc.
29 East 21st Street, New York, NY 10010

Produced for The Rosen Publishing Group, Inc. by Alix Wood Books
Written by Eloise Macgregor
Designed and illustrated by Alix Wood

Names: Macgregor, Eloise, author. | Wood, Alix, illustrator.
Title: A kid's guide to understanding vaccines / by Eloise Macgregor, illustrated by Alix Wood.
Description: New York : PowerKids Press, 2022. | Series: Be a virus warrior! | Includes glossary.
Identifiers: ISBN 9781725333017 (pbk.) | ISBN 9781725333031 (library bound) | ISBN 9781725333024 (6 pack) | ISBN 9781725333048 (ebook)
Subjects: LCSH: Vaccines--Juvenile literature. | Vaccination--Juvenile literature. | Viruses--Juvenile literature. | Virus diseases--Juvenile literature.
Classification: LCC RA638.M32 2022 | DDC 615.3'72--dc23

All illustrations © Alix Wood

Manufactured in the United States of America

CPSIA Compliance Information: Batch #CSPK22: For Further Information contact
Rosen Publishing, New York, New York at 1-800-237-9932

Find us on

In a time when children and parents are looking for information about COVID-19 and vaccines, I found the book *Be a Virus Warrior! A Kid's Guide to Understanding Vaccines* to be medically accurate, useful, and a good read. — Dr. Neil Winawer, Hospitalist and Professor of Medicine, Emory University School of Medicine.

Contents

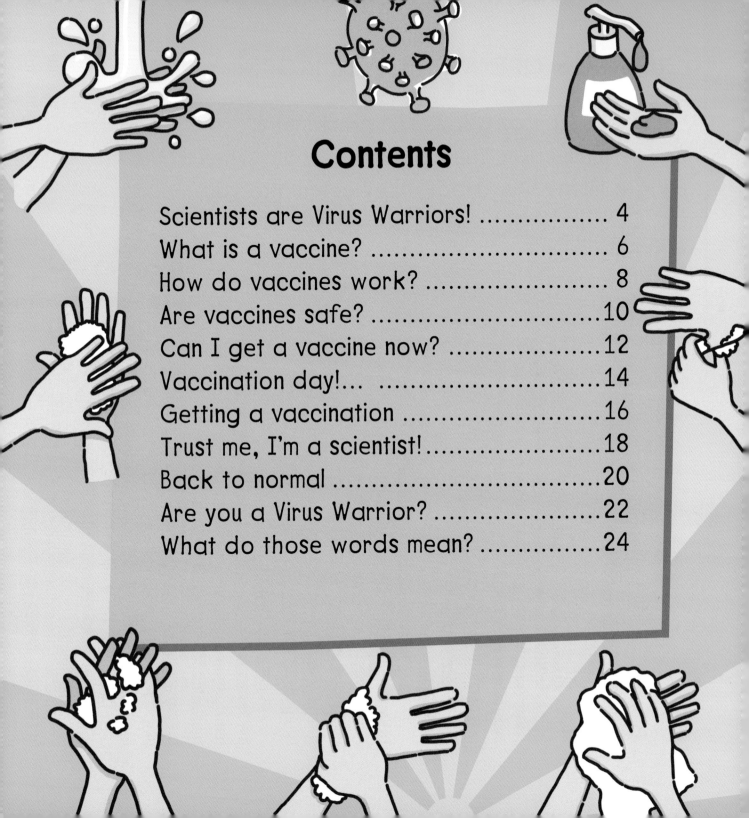

Scientists are Virus Warriors!

A virus is a type of **germ**. You can't see a virus germ because they are SO tiny! But when they get inside your body, they can make you sick. **COVID-19** is a new illness caused by a **coronavirus**.

A virus can spread from one person to another really easily. In just a few months, this coronavirus has spread all around the world!

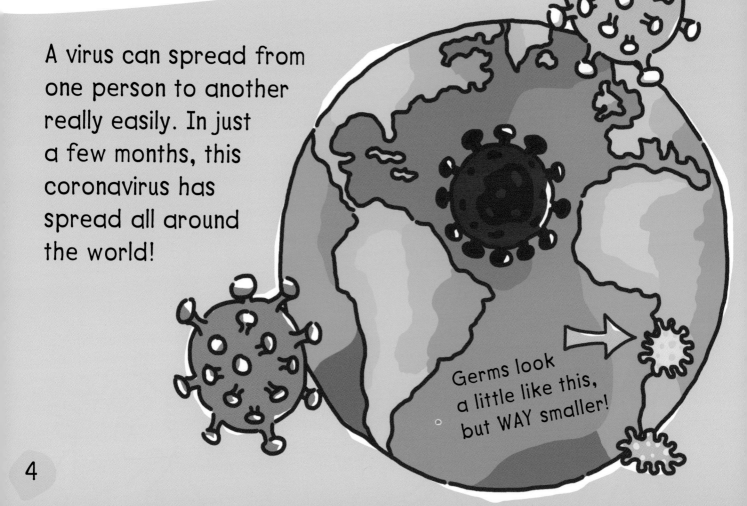

Germs look a little like this, but WAY smaller!

People are trying to keep away from each other to stop it from spreading—but we can't do that forever!

When there is a virus going around, scientists get to work. The best way to keep a virus from spreading is to protect everyone. How? Scientists create a **vaccine**!

5

What is a vaccine?

A vaccine is a specially made substance created by scientists that helps your body fight disease.

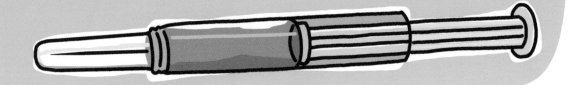

Edward Jenner invented the first vaccine to fight a horrible disease called **smallpox**.

Jenner heard that farmers who caught a milder disease called cowpox never got smallpox.

He made a vaccine with cowpox in it. He tested it to see if it might keep people from getting smallpox. It worked!

Now, millions of people's lives are saved every year by vaccines. You probably had some vaccines when you were a baby, to protect you from diseases such as measles and polio.

With a new virus, we may not already have a vaccine that can fight it. Scientists have to work hard to create a new one.

How do vaccines work?

Your body has tiny helpers that are part of your **immune system**. These disease-fighting **cells** are found all over your body. When they spot an invader, they get to work!

To make a vaccine, scientists examine the virus. They often look for weak, harmless parts of it that they can use to create a safe vaccine.

A vaccine teaches your immune system to recognize and fight the virus without making you sick.

After a vaccine, the next time your body spots those germs, it is ready to kill them all off, Warrior style!

After you've had the vaccine, you can still catch and spread COVID-19.

Your immune system makes the virus weaker and less able to spread, and it keeps YOU from getting sick.

9

Are vaccines safe?

Scientists have been creating vaccines for over 200 years. They are very good at it! And before doctors are allowed to give people a new vaccine, it has to go through LOTS of tests.

Everyone wanted scientists to work super fast to make the COVID-19 vaccine, but they still made sure it was completely safe. How?

Scientists in many different countries shared their information.

The people in charge made sure vaccine programs had enough money, quickly. Usually it takes AGES to raise enough money!

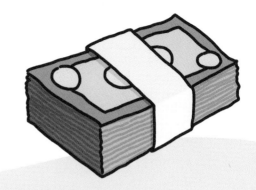

Ordinary people quickly agreed to help test the vaccine. It usually takes AGES to find people to test vaccines too.

Companies began making the vaccine, so it was ready to send out the moment it was **approved**.

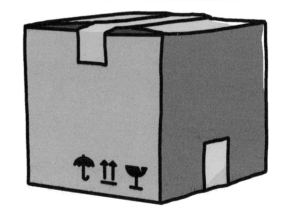

All these people have been real Virus Warrior heroes!

Can I get the vaccine now?

First, doctors **vaccinate** people who might get really sick if they catch a virus. With COVID-19, older people and people with other illnesses are usually at the top of the list, along with people who care for them.

It's great to know that people you love are now protected.

Essential workers who can't stay home might get the vaccine next.

Then, younger people will be offered the vaccine. Don't worry if you're told you can't have it. Some people can't if they have an **allergy**. Young children may not even need to be vaccinated. Your doctor will tell you if you need to have it.

If most people around you have had the vaccine, that will help protect you.

Vaccination day!

If you are invited for a vaccination, you might go to the doctor, a clinic, or perhaps a drugstore. People may even give the vaccine at your school.

You can do some things to get ready.

Wear a short-sleeved shirt, so it's easy to get to your upper arm.

Maybe pack a book to take with you, to keep you busy while you wait.

If you have little brothers or sisters, you could pretend to give their cuddly toy a vaccine. Then they'll know what to expect when they have theirs.

And their teddy bear will be protected too!

Getting a vaccination

The person giving the vaccine is an expert Virus Warrior. You may feel nothing or a tiny pinch, but it only lasts a split second. Some people get a slightly sore arm or a bit of a fever afterward.

That's perfectly normal. It shows your immune system is busy being a Virus Warrior!

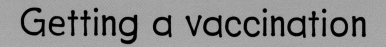

With many vaccines you need two shots a few weeks apart. It may take a few days after that before you are completely protected. Keep wearing a mask and keeping your distance until you are told you don't need to.

Then, you and your immune system are full members of the Virus Warrior Club!

Some people may not receive a vaccine. Don't make them feel bad. They may have a good reason.

Trust me, I'm a scientist!

Because COVID-19 is caused by a new virus, people are talking about it everywhere—on TV and on social media. Social media can be great, but it can also spread false information.

Get your information from the experts. Scientists and doctors who study viruses know the most about them. They are studying this new virus all the time.

Did you know that viruses change? That keeps scientists on their toes!

If the virus changes a lot, scientists will put their superhero capes back on and make a new vaccine.

19

Back to normal

Once most people have gotten the vaccine, the world can start to get back to normal. COVID-19 may still be around, but you can begin getting out and doing the things you enjoy.

Maybe have a party or a sleepover ...

... and go back to school and see your friends...

...or go on trips!

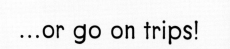

Perhaps go to a sports game, or the movies.

What are you looking forward to doing most?

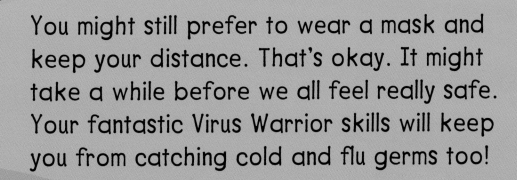

You might still prefer to wear a mask and keep your distance. That's okay. It might take a while before we all feel really safe. Your fantastic Virus Warrior skills will keep you from catching cold and flu germs too!

Are you a Virus Warrior?

Take this quiz to see if you have the power to be a Virus Warrior! The answers are at the bottom of page 24.

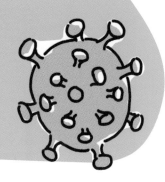

1. Who would you ask for information about vaccines?
   a) Doctors and scientists
   b) Aliens from outer space
   c) Some friends on social media

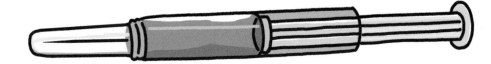

2. How do vaccines work?
   a) They give us the virus
   b) They teach our immune system to recognize and fight the virus
   c) They don't work

3. How do we know a vaccine is safe?
   a) Scientists do lots of tests on the vaccine
   b) Scientists have been making safe vaccines for hundreds of years
   c) both of the above reasons

4. Your doctor offers you the vaccine. Should you...?
   a) Go and get it. It will help keep you safe
   b) Worry it isn't safe, and don't get it.

A vaccine can turn your immune system into the ultimate Virus Warrior! Then you can get back to normal life!

What do those words mean?

allergy having a reaction such as sneezing, itching, or a rash.

approved accepted as safe.

cells tiny units of plant or animal life.

coronavirus a type of virus.

COVID-19 a new illness that can affect your lungs that is caused by a virus called coronavirus.

essential workers people who have jobs that are essential to society, such as teachers, nurses, and bus drivers.

germ a microscopic living thing that causes disease.

immune system the bodily system that protects the body from foreign substances.

smallpox a disease caused by a virus that causes a fever and skin rash.

vaccinate to give a vaccine, usually by injection.

vaccine a preparation given, often by injection, to keep you from getting a disease.

Quiz answers: 1. a, 2. b, 3. c, 4. a